D1196155

DISCOVERING WORLD CULTURES

DISCOVERING WORLD CULTURES

Crabtree Publishing Company

PMB 16A, 350 Fifth Avenue   612 Welland Avenue
Suite 3308   St. Catharines, Ontario
New York, NY 10118   L2M 5V6

Created by McRae Books Srl
© McRae Books Srl 2001

All rights reserved. No part of this publication may be
reproduced in any form without the prior
written permission of the publisher and the copyright owner.

Cataloging in Publication Data

MacDonald, Fiona, 1950-
   Food / Fiona MacDonald.
      p. cm. -- (Discovering world cultures)
   Includes index.
   ISBN 0-7787-0238-3 (RLB) -- ISBN 0-7787-0248-0 (pbk.)
   1. Food--History--Juvenile literature. [1.Food.] I. Title. II.
Series
   TX355 .M254 2001
   641.3'09--dc21
                                        00-065994
                                        LC

Coordinating Editor: Ellen Rodger
Production Coordinator: Rosie Gowsell
McRae Books Srl
Editors: Holly Willis, Anne McRae
Illustrations: Lorenzo Cecchi, Gian Paolo Faleschini, Antonella Pastorelli, Paola Ravaglia,
Studio Stalio (Alessandro Cantucci, Fabiano Fabbrucci, Andrea Morandi, Ivan Stalio)
Design: Marco Nardi, Adriano Nardi, Laura Ottina

Color separations: Litocolor, Florence, Italy
1234567890   Printed and bound in Italy by Nuova G.E.P.   0987654321

FOOD

Text by Fiona Macdonald

Illustrations by Gian paolo Faleschini, Antonella Pastorelli,
Paola Ravaglia, Studio Stalio

Crabtree
www.crabtreebooks.com

List of Contents

For survival
We all need to eat and drink to stay alive. Carbohydrate foods, such as bread, potatoes, and pasta (right), are used by our **digestive system** to make fuel for our bodies.

For energy
Carbohydrate foods provide energy. We need to eat a lot of them, to give our muscles power. Athletes eat plenty of rice or pasta while training. Some, like this runner, often eat a large carbohydrate meal hours before a big race.

Good food is...

Food is essential for life. Without food, we would die. In spite of this knowledge, food is a problem for many people today. In wealthy industrialized countries, many people eat too much, and are overweight. Some people worry so much about looking slim that they develop **eating disorders**. Children often eat too many sweet or salty junk foods. In developing countries, food problems are very different. There is more than enough food produced to feed everyone on the planet, yet people still go hungry and starve to death because of poverty, natural disasters, and wars.

Enjoyable
Eating foods that we like makes us feel good. But many of our favorite foods are not very good for us. They have too much sugar, fat, salt, and artificial flavor and color that are bad for our health. Even soft drinks can harm us if we drink too much of them. The acid in pop rots our teeth, and the sugar in them is fattening.

Traditionally, roast meat and red wine were popular foods in many parts of Europe. They were eaten with bread or potatoes, and green vegetables or a salad. The meat provided plenty of protein, vitamins, and minerals. A small amount of wine helped digestion and was also good for the heart.

This boy is sucking his favorite drink through a straw. It tastes good but it is bad for his teeth.

Varied
Traditionally, people ate food grown, hunted, or fished locally. The crops they grew, and the animals they hunted, were well-suited to their environment. For example, rice only grows in hot, wet climates, but oats and barley can survive short, cold summers. Bison are adapted to harsh prairie conditions in North America, but dairy cows thrive on green pasture. Different religious beliefs and social customs also influence peoples' choice of food. In some cultures, meat is reserved for men or for wealthy people. Poor people, women, and children eat cheaper food.

Some common crops: oats and rye, rice, wheat, barley, and corn.

Nourishing

Eating almost anything will stop us from feeling hungry, but foods are not all the same! They contain different amounts of nutrients, which our bodies use in different ways. Carbohydrates, found in bread, pasta, and potatoes, give us energy. Proteins, found in meat, fish, and beans, build strong bones. Fats, found in oil, butter, nuts, and cheese, keep our joints and brains working smoothly. Foods also contain small amounts of natural chemicals, known as vitamins and minerals. Vitamin D, found in milk, gives us strong bones and teeth. Vitamin C, found in fresh fruits and vegetables, protects us from infection. Iron forms healthy blood, and zinc is good for our skin and hair.

Fat

Protein

Fruit and vegetables

Carbohydrate

Flavors

There are foods that we enjoy eating, and foods that we choose not to eat. These preferences are not always the same for everyone! What is delicious to some, can taste awful to others. Often, our tastes change as we get older. Many children like foods that seem too sweet to adults. Older people often enjoy sour or bitter foods that young children hate.

Mouth, containing teeth and saliva which break down food.

Pharynx, links the mouth with the oesophagus.

Oesophagus, which carries food down to the stomach.

Liver, which makes bile salts to help digestion.

Stomach, where food is mixed with chemicals to break it down even more.

Gall bladder, where bile salts are stored, before being released into the stomach.

Pancreas, which makes digestive juices.

Colon, which absorbs water and minerals from food.

Appendix

Small intestine, where nutrients are absorbed into the body.

Anus, which expels waste matter.

Rectum, where waste matter is stored.

To be eaten in the right amounts

We need to eat a combination of foods to stay healthy. Scientists illustrate the ideal mixture of foods as a pyramid (above). We should eat a lot of the foods at the bottom of the pyramid, and a little of the foods at the top. We should also think carefully about the amount of food we eat. Too much food, even if it is the right kind of food, will make us overweight. Being overweight is not healthy. It strains our heart, joints, and digestion. It can even shorten our lives!

Easy to digest

Our bodies have to digest, or break down food before we can absorb all the nourishment it contains. Digestion begins in our mouths, where we chew food into a paste with our teeth, and mix it with **saliva**. The chewed food then passes into our stomach, where it mixes with more chemicals, and is slowly pushed along the whole of our **alimentary canal**. It finally leaves our bodies as waste.

For many people, doughnuts are tasty. They are soft, sticky, and very sweet, but not very healthy. Doughnuts have too much sugar, and are fried in fat. We should eat these foods occasionally, and not every day!

The ancient Egyptians decorated their tombs with scenes of everyday life, including eating, drinking, farming, and catching food. These Egyptian boatmen (above) are using nets to catch fish from the Nile River .

In ancient times

People first began to live in villages, and farm the surrounding land, around 10,000 years ago, in the Middle East. This changed the way people ate. Their diets became based on grains instead of wild food that they hunted and gathered locally. Despite the change in the way they lived, people still ate meals of meat they had hunted or trapped, and fish they caught in rivers or the sea.

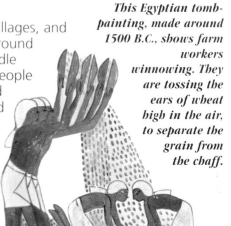

This Egyptian tomb-painting, made around 1500 B.C., shows farm workers winnowing. They are tossing the ears of wheat high in the air, to separate the grain from the chaff.

Producing food

Most of the foods we eat today have a very long history. Some, like wheat, which is used to make bread, have been grown for almost 10,000 years. In the past, producing food was so important that people, in most parts of the world were farmers, or made a living from work connected to farming. Until 1750, farmers had only hand-tools or horse-drawn machinery to help them. After this time, new machines were invented, to let farmers work the land quickly and more efficiently. In the 20th century, new **chemicals** were introduced, designed to feed growing crops and protect them from pests and diseases. Today, in many parts of the world, farming is big business, controlled by wealthy landowners and **multinational companies**.

A fisherman (left), with his catch from the sea, was painted on the walls of a palace on the Greek island of Thera around 2500 B.C.

This medieval peasant is preparing a field for planting wheat. He is digging furrows, which are hollows where the seed will be planted, using a plow drawn by oxen.

As a farmer

Over the centuries, different crops, suited to different environments, were **domesticated** around the world. In the past, most farmworkers were peasants, and grew only enough food for their families. Sometimes, farmers had to work on land belonging to a powerful **lord**, as in ancient China or Egypt.

At harvest time

Traditionally in farming areas, the harvest was the most important time of the year. Men, women, and children worked together to harvest a crop and put it in barns for storage. Everyone knew that their lives depended on cooperation and good weather. If workers were not quick enough, or if rains came and ruined the crop, there would be no food to eat during the coming year.

This picture shows medieval people hard at work at harvest time. They are cutting wheat with special curved knives called sickles.

Using technology

During the nineteenth century, new technology changed farming. Machines allowed farmers to grow and harvest more crops with less manpower. The horse-drawn reaping machine (left) was designed to help farmers on isolated prairie farms at harvest time. By the end of the century, steam-powered traction engines and reaping machines made farm work a little easier.

Today, most cows are milked by machines, but this farmer milked her cow the old way, by hand.

This reaper (above) was first used in the 1840s in the U.S.

Such as livestock

Sheep, goats, and cattle have been domesticated since around 5,000 B.C. Traditionally, different **breeds** were kept for different purposes. Some provided milk, and others provided meat. Sheeps' wool was used for clothing. Their meat was eaten as mutton or lamb. The skins from sheep, cattle and goats were **tanned** to make leather.

Such as dairy products

Female cows, sheep, and goats all produce milk to feed their young. For over 7,000 years, farmers and dairyworkers have collected this milk, and sold it for drinking, or used it to make butter and cheese. Butter is made by churning cow's milk until the butterfat it contains sticks together in a lump. Cheese is made by curdling, or souring milk from sheep, goats, and cows, so that it separates into solids, called curds, and liquid, called whey. The curds are then salted and pressed to make cheese.

Sheep have grazed on the mountain pastures of the Piedmont region of northern Italy for hundreds of years.

This little boy in China is holding a huge turnip grown in the family garden.

This diagram shows environmentally friendly methods of farming. Different crops are grown to keep the soil fertile, and animal manure is used instead of fertilizer. Tiny insects called aphids, which damage crops, are eaten by ladybugs instead of being killed with pesticides. Cattle can graze on fresh grass instead of being fed artificial food pellets. The food grows and ripens naturally, and is sold at local markets.

Using sustainable methods

During the 1980s and 1990s, many farmers in Europe and North America began to distrust modern farming methods. These methods rely heavily on **fertilizers** and **pesticides**. Instead, they called for a return to traditional methods, such as farmyard manure, **crop rotation**, and the use of insect predators to eat pests. Many farmers began to farm organically, using methods that were **sustainable**. Their produce was popular with shoppers, and sold for high prices.

By preserving it

Fish was one of the first foods to be caught and eaten by people who lived thousands of years ago. Fresh fish spoils very quickly, and cannot be stored. Today, most fish are frozen, but in the past, they were preserved by being smoked over wood fires (left), or packed in jars or barrels, surrounded by layers of salt. Many people still enjoy eating smoked and salted fish today.

Preparing and cooking food

Preparing and cooking food can be difficult work. It can also be a way of showing guests, friends, and family members how much they are welcomed and cared for. Preparing a meal can be a creative act, or a labor of love. An old saying declares that: "The way to a man's heart is through his stomach!" In the past, women were usually responsible for cooking for their families. Sometimes they had servants to help them, but women, rich and poor, did the meal shopping, planning, cooking, and serving.

Cassava flour is an important food for the rainforest peoples of South America. It is prepared from the roots of the plant. They are soaked in water, dried, and then crushed (above).

Using tools

Cooks use many different **utensils** when preparing food. They range from simple spoons and knives to special equipment like this stone quern (left), used for grinding grain. Querns have been used for over 3,000 years. They are made of two flat stones, with a space for grain in between. As the top stone is turned around, it crushes the grain against the lower one, producing flour.

Many different grains are grown for food, including wheat, oats, barley, corn, millet and sorghum. They must be processed before cooking. This woman (above) is separating grain from the chaff.

In ancient times

Some cooking methods have changed very little over the centuries. This little statue (right) was made in Egypt around 2,000 BC. It shows a man grilling meat over a charcoal fire. This is exactly how meat is cooked in a modern barbecue. The cook holds a fan in his left hand to shield his face from the heat of the fire and to fan the flames.

By baking it

Bread is a **staple** food in many parts of Europe, North America, and the Middle East. It is made by mixing wheat flour with water, and baking it. Usually, yeast and sometimes salt, is added along with the water. The yeast makes the bread rise and gives it a light, spongy texture. The salt adds flavor. Some people make bread at home, but most people in **developed countries** buy bread from professional bakers, like this one, pictured above.

The traditional way

Many beliefs and traditions have developed around food preparation. In some European countries, people believe that it is unlucky to see crossed knives on a table, or to spill salt. Other ancient beliefs center around the place where food is cooked. In China, for example, many families display an image of the god Tsao Chun (right) in their kitchens. He watches the family's behavior, and reports any wrong-doings to heaven at the end of each year. Traditionally, it is believed that people will be rewarded or punished, because of these reports.

For fun

These children (above) are preparing a meal of spaghetti and salad. Today, many boys and girls like to learn how to cook meals and snacks for themselves and their families. Young cooks have become famous television personalities, starring in their own shows.

Using meat

Meat is almost always served cooked. Cooking kills germs the meat might contain and makes it tastier to eat. Tender cuts from the breast or rump of an animal cook quickly but meat lower down on the legs is tougher and needs long, slow cooking. Meat is usually expensive, so cooks use trimmings from larger cuts of meat, mixed with salt and spices, to make cheaper sausages (left) or pies.

These people are making traditional sausages, mincing the meat and squeezing it into skins.

Microwave ovens, like this one (above) from the 1950s, can cook food in minutes, but early ovens, such as these Ancient Roman ones (below), took a long time to heat up, and were much less convenient.

In the kitchen

In the past, the kitchen was often "the heart of the home" as can be seen from this seventeenth century Dutch painting (below). The whole family spent much of the day there, keeping warm around the kitchen fire. For women, kitchens were always places of work, but for men, they were places where they could eat, drink, and relax.

Using ovens

Fire has been used to cook food for thousands of years. Other forms of heat can also be used for cooking. Many modern stoves are powered by electricity. They cook food in very hot air. Microwave ovens, were first invented in 1948. They cook by generating waves of invisible energy that pass through food, raising it to high temperatures very quickly.

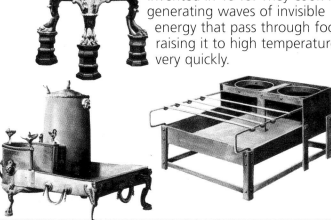

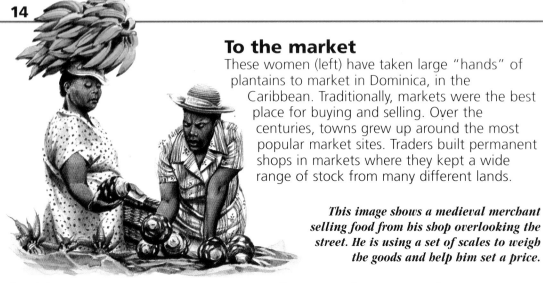

To the market

These women (left) have taken large "hands" of plantains to market in Dominica, in the Caribbean. Traditionally, markets were the best place for buying and selling. Over the centuries, towns grew up around the most popular market sites. Traders built permanent shops in markets where they kept a wide range of stock from many different lands.

This image shows a medieval merchant selling food from his shop overlooking the street. He is using a set of scales to weigh the goods and help him set a price.

The journey food makes

It would not be surprising to find that many children have no idea that eggs are laid by hens or that milk comes from a cow. Most people in **developed countries** live far away from the places where food is produced, and do not know anything about how the food made it to their table. Instead, they take it for granted that they will be able to buy whatever they want in shops and supermarkets. People expect to find fresh fruits and vegetables on sale all year round, whatever the season. People also like to buy new and different produce from many parts of the world. The food in markets today travels a great distance before it reaches our local market.

To the supermarket

Supermarkets are a recent invention. In the past, shoppers purchased different kinds of goods from specialty stores, run by butchers, bakers, grocers, and produce sellers. Workers in these shops, like the bakers (below), were often very knowledgeable about the goods they sold. They also got to know their regular customers well.

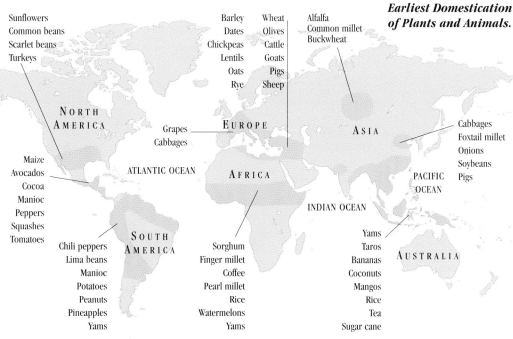

Earliest Domestication of Plants and Animals.

Sunflowers, Common beans, Scarlet beans, Turkeys

NORTH AMERICA

Maize, Avocados, Cocoa, Manioc, Peppers, Squashes, Tomatoes

Grapes, Cabbages

Barley, Dates, Chickpeas, Lentils, Oats, Rye — Wheat, Olives, Cattle, Goats, Pigs, Sheep

EUROPE

Alfalfa, Common millet, Buckwheat

ASIA

Cabbages, Foxtail millet, Onions, Soybeans, Pigs

ATLANTIC OCEAN

AFRICA

PACIFIC OCEAN

INDIAN OCEAN

Chili peppers, Lima beans, Manioc, Potatoes, Peanuts, Pineapples, Yams

SOUTH AMERICA

Sorghum, Finger millet, Coffee, Pearl millet, Rice, Watermelons, Yams

Yams, Taros, Bananas, Coconuts, Mangos, Rice, Tea, Sugar cane

AUSTRALIA

From all over the world

The first farming villages began in the Middle East almost 10,000 years ago. People living there grew early forms of wheat and barley and herded sheep and goats. Potatoes were first **cultivated** in the Andes mountains of South America. Rice was first grown in China. Corn was grown in Central America, and African farmers grew millet. Today, **third world** farmers are abandoning these old crops that are well suited to their environment. Instead, they grow new "cash crops," such as flowers or **exotic** vegetables to be sent to market in wealthy parts of the world. .

And transportation

Food is grown on farms in the country and must be taken to market in towns and cities, where most people live. In the past, perishable foods, such as milk and vegetables, could only be carried for short distances, in simple carts like this one from China (below). In Southeast Asia food is still sold from boats at special floating markets (left).

Refrigerators were introduced in the 1920s but they were very expensive. They changed food storage. Foods such as milk and cooked meats, could now be kept cold enough to prevent spoilage. Refrigerators also changed shopping habits. In the past, shoppers bought foods fresh every day. Fridges allowed people to buy food once or twice a week.

Following trade routes

Food has been sold or traded to different parts of the world for over 2,000 years. Until the 19th century, most of this trade was local. Only the rarest, most valuable foods, such as herbs and spices, were worth the cost of transporting around the world. In the 1800s, fast ships, powered by sail and steam, were built in Europe and North America. These ships made it affordable to transport **commodities** from many distant countries. Tea from China and India was shipped to Britain and Europe. Sugar from the Caribbean was shipped all over the world.

Seasonal foods like fruit are often processed before being sold. The most common ways of processing are freezing, canning, and drying. Processing keeps food in good condition for several months. Processing fruit such as kiwi (below) in New Zealand, prevents waste at harvest, when all the farm produce ripens at the same time. Canned fruits and vegetables are not as nutritious as fresh ones but they are still very good for us.

This Indian trader (left) has over a hundred spices on display in his shop. Many of the spices are very valuable, and are weighed carefully before being sold.

In packaging

Today, food often has to travel long distances to reach grocery stores, so it has to be well protected, or it will rot. Sometimes, fruits and vegetables are chilled, or packed before transportation. Sometimes, they are harvested and packed before they are ripe, so that they will not rot. This helps fruits and vegetables stay in better condition, but many people think it spoils their flavor.

These workers (right) are carefully packing lettuce in big cardboard boxes on a farm in California. The lettuce will be shipped to market all over North America.

That is processed

During the 20th century, people in North America often felt that they had no time to cook. They were too busy at work, or too tired after work. They relied on **convenience foods** such as sugar-coated breakfast cereals and canned soup. As you can see from this cereal box (left) and soup can (right), processed foods are often packaged in bright colors, to attract the attention of shoppers as they walk through supermarkets.

This image of a Campbell's soup can, was an inspiration for 20th century American artist Andy Wharbol.

Fast and slow food

Historians often describe the late 20th century as a time of "instant gratification". This means that people did not want to wait for the things that they wanted, or to work towards achieving a goal over time. People wanted everything to happen immediately, from promotion at work to satisfying their hunger. In the past it took a long time to prepare a good meal. Bread needed to rise for at least four hours, and wine took months or even years to make. By the 1970s, many people were not prepared to wait so long. They preferred to purchase food that was already prepared from supermarkets and restaurants. It did not matter to them that this fast food was often not healthy.

On the street

Fast food, bought from vendors on the street, is popular in many countries. People can "grab a bite to eat" as they rush from place to place. These street vendors (below), who carry their food in baskets on their bicycles, sell food in Nepal.

Like sandwiches

Fast food, like this triple-decker sandwich, is a speciality in many North American restaurants, but the first sandwich was just a piece of cold roast meat between two slices of bread. It was invented in the 18th century by an English **nobleman**, the Earl of Sandwich. He was a gambler, who did not like to miss a single game of cards, so he asked his servants to bring him a quick snack at the card table instead. The sandwich was named after him.

This drive-in in the U.S. is shaped like an enormous hotdog so that it will catch the attention of passing drivers.

Sold at drive-Ins

Drive-ins are fast food restaurants where diners do not even have to get out of their car. Instead, their food is served to them in take out bags or on trays. Drive-ins first became popular in the 1950s in the U.S. By then, most people had cars, and liked to spend their leisure time "cruising" along the highways. Drive-in restaurants were fast and convenient for motorists.

Before photography was invented, wealthy people had their portraits painted. This painting (above) was completed in 1586 and shows all the members of a wealthy family saying grace before eating their meal.

With the family

In the past, families gathered together for the main meal of the day. Eating together was an important part of family life. By sharing food and talking about the day's events, families grew closer.

Using fresh ingredients

Preparing food at home can be quick. It only takes about five minutes to cook an omelet. Often, cooking a meal at home can take much longer. Even so, home cooking is still very popular, and books by writers like Rosalba Gioffrè in Italy (right), or Martha Stewart, are bestsellers. Home cooked food is usually fresher than anything bought in a store, and does not usually contain artificial flavors or **preservatives**.

As a hobby

Throughout history, preparing food was simply a necessity because our bodies require food. Today, in developed countries, cooking has become a popular hobby, done for the pleasure of mixing, chopping, and baking ingredients, rather than just for eating. People enjoy doing something creative, like this girl (left), who has made cookies. Other people find cooking a way to relax.

With friends

For many people, sharing a meal with friends is one of the best ways to relax. By sitting down together with plenty of time to talk, friends can get to know each other and learn to trust each other.

This painting by French painter Auguste Renoir is called "The Boating Party". It shows people enjoying food and talking with their friends.

During war time

During the Second World War (1939-1945), there were food shortages in many parts of Europe, and fresh foods, such as meat, were almost impossible to buy. Soldiers needed food that was **nourishing**, was easy to store and carry, and did not have to be cooked. Governments ordered supplies of ready-to-eat food, such as "Spam" (Spiced Pork And Ham) in a can, which could be stored for years, but was ready in minutes.

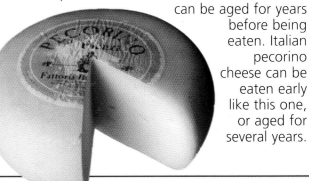

Can take years

Some foods can take years before they are ready to eat. They need time to mature and develop their flavor. Certain varieties of cheese can be aged for years before being eaten. Italian pecorino cheese can be eaten early like this one, or aged for several years.

From fish

Caviar is a famous **delicacy**, enjoyed in many lands. Only wealthy people can afford it, because it is very expensive. It is not a complicated dish. It is simply the salted eggs of the sturgeon fish. Caviar is black and shiny, and tastes fishy and salty. It is usually eaten cold, as a party appetizer with toast, or at the beginning of a meal. Caviar is becoming scarce because overfishing and pollution are killing off the sturgeon.

Are often salty

Some people like the taste of potato chips and other salty snacks. They crave salty flavorings, such as soy sauce, in their food. This taste for salt is ancient and may have helped early humans survive. Our ancestors learned to like salt, because it is essential for life. People who are active, or live in hot climates lose salt in sweat. This salt needs to be replaced. Too much salt, however, is very bad for us, and can lead to disease.

All things nice

Taste is a very **individual** sensation, and few people react to the same foods in exactly the same way. Scientists have discovered that all food flavors are a mixture of four main tastes: sweet, salty, bitter, and sour. Some people enjoy sour foods, such as pickles, or tangy lemon drinks. Some prefer bitter tastes. These are usually blended with other flavors, as in dark-roasted coffee, or spicy foods. But most people prefer just two of the four main tastes: sweet or salty. Color, texture, and temperature can also be very important in what makes food appealing to an individual. Do you like the crisp crunchiness of apples, or the smooth stickiness of chocolate cake? Are you attracted by bright red strawberries or yellow bananas? Do you prefer hot soup or cold ice cream?

This woman is holding a tray of freshly-baked salted pretzels.

Pizza is popular around the world but it first came from Italy. The recipe was carried across the Atlantic in the early 20th century by immigrants moving to North America.

Can be sweet

Some people prefer sweet-tasting foods. Sugar is often called an "empty" food. It is high in calories, but contains no other nutrients. For this reason, sweet foods are often eaten only at the end of a meal, after a main course, or as special treats. Too much sugar can be bad for us. It is absorbed very quickly by the body, leading to sudden highs and lows of energy and emotions. Sugar also helps create **bacteria** that rot our teeth.

Becoming international

Today's world is sometimes called a "global village." We know more about other peoples' cultures, fashions, and foods because of high speed travel, and communication systems such as radio, TV, and the Internet. Foods that once belonged to only one region are now available worldwide.

These sugary marzipan fruits are traditionally made in Italy as a treat, especially at Easter when they are shaped into animals.

Like chocolate cake

Cakes, baked from eggs, sugar, butter, and flour, are popular in many countries. They are often eaten at birthday parties or on special occasions. Chocolate cakes are a special favorite because they are rich and sweet. Chocolate melts at mouth-temperature due to its high fat content.

Can be a novelty

Popular foods are often fun to eat. They may have interesting shapes or be easy to hold like "finger food," which does not require a knife, fork, or plate. Hamburgers, hot dogs, potato chips, and french fries can all be eaten easily, at parties, picnics, barbecues, or in the street. But be warned! Novelty food is often not healthy.

Shish kebabs (right) first came from Turkey. They are made of meat and vegetables threaded on a skewer, brushed with oil, sprinkled with herbs, then grilled. You eat them by biting off pieces with your teeth. They are one kind of fun food that is healthy to eat!

Depends on the point of view

There is no world wide standard of good taste in food. It all depends on each diner's point of view. As children, we learn from our parents, and others close to us, what is good to eat, and what is not. For example, many people from North America shudder at the thought of eating ants, a forest food that is popular in many lands. They would be surprised to know that ants actually taste moist, sweet, and crunchy!

Insects and other small animals are favorite foods for people who still follow hunter-gatherer lifestyles. In Australia, Aborigines dig for wichety grubs. In the Amazon rainforests, people eat some kinds of spiders. This man (above) from Borneo, is digging for ants.

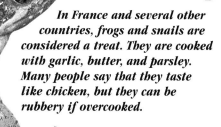

In France and several other countries, frogs and snails are considered a treat. They are cooked with garlic, butter, and parsley. Many people say that they taste like chicken, but they can be rubbery if overcooked.

In many colors

We often enjoy foods that are very colorful, such as this scooped-out melon piled high with juicy fruits (above). All fresh fruits and vegetables are good for us, but many people prefer fruit, because of its naturally sweet taste. The colors in fruits and vegetables can sometimes give us clues as to the nutrients they contain. For example, the bright orange color in carrots comes from Beta-Carotene, which helps produce Vitamin A. Some people think that we are attracted to colorful foods because our ancient ancestors discovered that eating them led to good health.

At Christmas
In Germany and Scandinavia, at Christmas time, people make houses (right) of gingerbread and candy. Children break off pieces and eat them as a special treat.

In Mexico, the Christian festival All Souls Day is celebrated on November 2, as the "Day of the Dead." Families visit the tombs of dead relatives, and give skull-shaped candy to children (left).

At New Year
In China, many different festivals are celebrated with traditional food. How the food looks is as important as the taste. Festival food is often beautifully arranged, like the platter of fruits and candies (above), prepared for New Year's Day. The cook has made a feast for the eyes, as well as the stomach!

Food festivals

All around the world, food is a **symbol** of life and prosperity. Many festivals are celebrated with special kinds of food, or with elaborate meals. The food served at celebrations varies from place to place, according to the local ingredients and to the wealth of the people celebrating. Often these foods include rare or expensive ingredients that are not eaten every day. The food may also be beautifully decorated with traditional designs that have special meanings. Sometimes the designs are religious; sometimes, they just express joy, or wishes for good luck. In many cultures, the spirits of dead families are not forgotten and foods are offered to them, to make sure that they continue to watch over family members still living.

For a marriage
In many cultures, marriages are celebrated with special meals. In Britain, this meal was traditionally called a "Wedding Breakfast," whatever time of the day it was held. The celebration included a wedding cake which was cut by the new couple together, as a sign of their shared future life. In ancient Israel (below) wedding feasts could last for a whole week, if the bride and bridegroom's family could afford it. Guests were entertained with the best food and wine and dancing.

To remember the dead
Roman men and women enjoyed dinner parties and banquets, and they believed the spirits of the dead were also able to share food in the world of the dead. Romans decorated graves and sarcophagi, or stone burial chests, (above) with carvings of people feasting. They prepared special meals in honor of dead family members at the festival of Parentalia, held each February.

On birthdays

In many countries, each person has a birthday; a special day each year to celebrate their life, or the life of the **saint** after whom they are named. Children, and adults, like to celebrate their birthday with parties. Special cakes (right) are baked and are usually decorated with candles, one for each year of the person's life. Some people say it brings good luck to blow out all the candles with one breath!

Presents of food are often a sign of peace and friendship. Left, a Macedonian woman offers walnuts from her tree to a soldier from the United Nations Peacekeeping Force.

In the streets

Food is sometimes carried through the streets as part of festival **processions**. Women from Bali, in Indonesia (right) are carrying offerings of food, incense, flowers, and water to local temples, as part of the annual Galungan festival. They offer food and gifts to the spirits of their ancestors who they believe come back to earth at festival time.

This illustration shows what the first Thanksgiving might have looked like.

At Thanksgiving

In 1620, the **Pilgrims** arrived in North America. The **colonists** were hoping to make a new life, but when they arrived it was nearly winter. They would have died from cold and hunger if Native Americans had not shown them how to find and grow food. One year later the Pilgrims held a special meal to give thanks to God for their first harvest, and invited the Native Americans to join them. North Americans have celebrated Thanksgiving Day ever since, with a special meal in late autumn. Favorite Thanksgiving foods include roast turkey, cranberry sauce, and pumpkin pie.

At Easter

For **Christians**, Easter is the most important religious festival of the year. It marks the time when Jesus Christ, who they believed was God's son on earth, was **crucified**. Christians believe that Jesus rose from the dead three days later, and that they, too, will live after death if they obey God's laws. Many different kinds of food are eaten at Easter. Eggs, an ancient **pagan** symbol of springtime and rebirth, are an Easter food because they **symbolize** new life. Children receive chocolate eggs as gifts, and beautifully painted hard-boiled eggs form part of celebration meals on Easter Day.

Pane con l'ova (bread with eggs) from Sicily, is made at Easter.

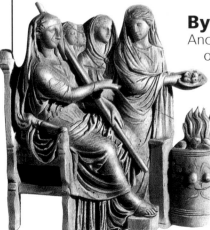

By ancient Romans

Ancient Greeks and Romans made sacrifices or offerings of food to their gods and goddesses. They believed that this would encourage the gods to help them. This Roman statue (left) shows a group of **priestesses** making an offering of food to the goddess Vesta, guardian of the hearth and home.

In Jainism

Followers of Jainism **anoint** enormous stone statues of Lord Bahubali, an important figure in their religion. Gifts of food are given to these statues in memory of Lord Bahubali's wisdom and **noble** actions. This Jain in India (above) is sprinkling the statue with flowers and is offering fruit and coconuts.

Offerings to the gods

Most cultures follow some form of religion, or set of **spiritual beliefs** and practices. Often, these practices involve making offerings of food to a **deity** or to ancestors. Sometimes this is done in the belief that the deity or ancestors will be able to enjoy the food and share in a celebration. People hope that offering food will keep the spirits happy so that they protect people on earth and send them good luck. Often, crops are placed on **alters** simply to give thanks for a good harvest and having enough to eat. Food can also be **symbolic**. The shape of the food might be thought to bring **fertility** and good fortune to people.

In Japan

Shintoism is one of the two ancient religions followed by Japanese people The other is Buddhism. Shinto worshipers, like this woman leave offerings of food at jinya, or shrines, as gifts for the kami, divine spirits that live there. Shinto shrines are usually built in places of natural beauty. The Japanese believe that beauty, like good food, pleases the spirits.

By Hindus

This beautifully made statue (above) portrays the Hindu god Ganesh, one of the three great Hindu gods. His elephant head represents intelligence and strength. A popular god, his statues stand in many temples, where they receive offerings of food, candies, and drink. In 1995, worshipers at temples in Delhi, Hong Kong, and London, reported that statues of Ganesh were drinking milk. Scientists tried to explain it, but no one knows what really happened.

For fertility

This doll (left), made from corn, beads, and plant fibers, belonged to a young woman in Cameroon, West Africa. Traditionally, plant-dolls were believed to make women fertile. The community could only survive if the land produced good crops, and if women had many children.

According to Roman myths and legends, Romulus and Remus, twin brothers who founded Rome, were nursed by a female wolf (below). She found them abandoned and hungry, and cared for them. Their food as babies had given them the characteristics of wolves. The brothers were especially brave and fierce.

Of forbidden foods

People from many faiths often choose to go without food at certain times of the year. They do this to show their faith and love for God. For example, **Muslims** do not eat or drink in daylight hours during the holy month of Ramadan, and Christians often promise to give up their favorite foods for Lent, the 40 days before Easter.

In Hebrew law

For thousands of years, many Jewish people have followed ancient laws recorded in their holy book, the **Torah**, that set out the foods they can and cannot eat. The food laws are called "kosher," which means "proper." Pigs, shellfish, and insects are forbidden, as is the mixing of milk and meat at the same meal. Animals to be eaten must be slaughtered using a method that allows the blood to drain out of their body, as shown above in this illustration of a 15th century Italian slaughterhouse.

Hindus in India believe that the cow is a sacred animal, and must not be killed or eaten. Cows are allowed to wander freely through villages, and even to hold up traffic in towns.

Zoroastrians follow the Prophet Zoroaster, who lived in ancient Persia. He taught that the world was locked in a struggle between the power of goodness, called Ahura Mazda, and the force of evil, called Angra Mainyu. To help goodness flourish in the world, Zoroastrians perform a special ceremony, called Jashan, giving thanks to Ahura Mazda, and asking for blessings. Zoroastrian priests call on the "Bounteous Immortals:" fruits and flowers, wine, water, and milk.

Offerings of oranges are left at a Buddhist temple in Singapore. You can also see photographs of ancestors to whom the oranges are being offered.

In China

At Chinese New Year, many families put out plates of oranges, or sometimes, red apples, in their homes. Red and orange are colors associated with good fortune, long life, and energy. People also visit Buddhist temples and make offerings to their family's ancestors, as a sign of respect. People often offer oranges stacked in the shape of a pyramid. The pyramid symbolizes being closer to heaven, because it raises the fruit towards the sky.

Without the potato

Potatoes first came from South America. During the 18th and 19th centuries, they were planted in Europe and replaced many traditional crops. Poor peasant farmers found that they were a valuable food source. An acre of potatoes could feed four times as many people as an acre of grain. In the 1840s, disaster struck, especially in Ireland. Potato crops were destroyed by plant disease, and millions of people starved.

This farm family eating a meal, was painted by a Dutch artist in 1885. Their only food was milk, bacon, and potatoes. This kept them alive, but left them without many essential vitamins and minerals.

Food problems

Food is a source of great pleasure for many people, but it can also cause many problems. Foods can be dangerous if they transmit disease. People often do not trust foods if they are new, strange, or **genetically modified.** An unbalanced diet, made up of just a few foods may satisfy hunger, but fail to provide the vitamins and minerals needed for good health. Too much food can be bad for our health, but too little food can be worse. Throughout history, wars and natural disasters have led to hunger, disease, and starvation.

Oranges, lemons, and limes are good sources of Vitamin C.

Caused by politics

In the late 1920s, **Communist** leader Josef Stalin launched a series of "five year plans" to reorganize industry and agriculture throughout the USSR, the Union of Soviet Socialist Republics. Peasants were forced to give up their family farms and work together in huge "collectives." All farming decisions were made by Communist officials. Crops failed and there was a terrible famine. Over 10 million people died.

Lacking vitamins

In the past, sailors often developed scurvy, a deadly illness caused by lack of Vitamin C. Sailors had no way of keeping fruit or vegetables fresh on long voyages. In the 18th century, a British ship's captain discovered that scurvy could be cured by lime juice, and made sure that he took a good supply of it on all his voyages.

Unemployed workers in the U.S. (right) line up for free meals at a soup kitchen run by a charity, during the Great Depression.

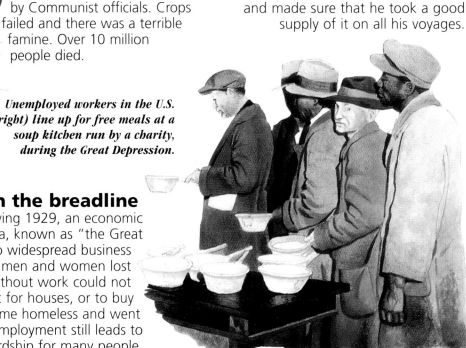

On the breadline

In the years following 1929, an economic crisis in North America, known as "the Great Depression," led to widespread business failures. Millions of men and women lost their jobs. People without work could not afford to pay rent for houses, or to buy food. Families became homeless and went hungry. Today, unemployment still leads to hunger and hardship for many people.

A peasant worker in the Ukraine (above) harvests grain in the 1930s. Shortages of seeds, fertilizer, and tools made farming difficult.

The black market

In times of war, food is often very scarce. Sometimes it is rationed, or limited by governments, to make sure that everyone gets a fair share. Sometimes a "black market" develops. A black market is an unofficial way of selling food outside a government's ration system. It means that people with money can buy extra, while poor people remain hungry. As this poster from France during World War II (1939–1945) points out, black markets are a "crime against the community."

Thousands of cows had to be killed in Britain in the 1990s, to try and stop the spread of "Mad Cow Disease." No one knows for sure how cows first became sick, but it was probably from eating animal remains added to their food, a cheaper source of food than grass.

And eating disorders

Normally, the amount of food we eat is naturally controlled by our brain. When we have eaten enough, it stops us feeling hungry again for several hours. Sometimes, this system does not work, and people develop eating disorders. They may eat a lot, even though they are not hungry or refuse to eat anything at all, in the mistaken belief that they are overweight. Doctors are not certain what causes these problems, but they may be connected to the desire for unnaturally thin body shapes.

Caused by disease

Foods usually keep us healthy, but occasionally they may cause disease. Bacteria that cause food poisoning, or pollution in the environment can make food bad. Occasionally, food products from diseased animals can pass an illness on to humans. During the 1980s and 1990s, meat from cows suffering from a brain disease known as "Mad Cow Disease," infected some humans in Europe with a similar fatal illness, "Creutzfeld-Jacob Disease".

This model (left), has a tape-measure around her chest, waist, and hips. These measurements vary greatly from person to person.

This African mother (right) and her three young children are malnourished because of a famine.

Dolly the sheep, born in 1997 in Scotland, was the first mammal ever cloned.

In poor countries

The wealth of the world today is unfairly divided. Some areas, such as North America and Europe, are very rich. Others, such as Africa, are extremely poor. This poverty leads to hunger, and, in some cases, famine, but it is not the only cause of food shortages. Governments often cut off their enemies' supplies on purpose, hoping that starvation will help defeat them. Farming in poor countries is difficult because they often cannot afford to educate people, or buy farm machinery. Natural disasters, such as floods or droughts, also kill crops.

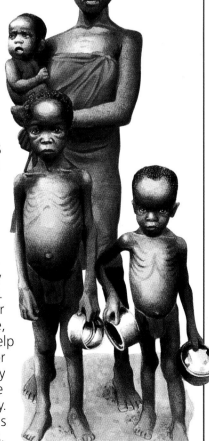

Modern science

During the 1990s, scientists made great advances in understanding the structure of genes, the basic "building blocks" of all living **cells**. Scientists experimented and changed the natural growth of crops. They believed that GMOs, **genetically modified organisms**, would be more productive and easier to grow. Although they claim that GMOs are completely safe, many people do not agree. People do not want to eat these unnatural foods and worry that genes from GMOs might mix with normal crops or wild plants with dangerous results.

For strength
Sometimes people eat a lot of food to help them put on weight to do their jobs. Weightlifters eat to build large muscles. Japanese Sumo wrestlers eat special high fat diets and follow strict rules when using the force of their heavy bodies to overpower their opponents.

These Sumo wrestlers in Japan compete against one another to see who is the most skillful at overpowering his opponent.

Salads are full of vitamins and minerals which can help prevent diseases.

Food and lifestyle

In any culture where food is plentiful and people do not eat just to survive, food means more than just nourishment. Religious or moral beliefs play a role in determining what foods can and cannot be eaten. For example, Jains believe they should not harm any living thing, so they do not eat animal flesh, or plants that die when you harvest them. Athletes need high energy foods that build muscle strength such as meat and pasta. Social changes also have a great affect on how much people eat. At various times in the past, both overeating and not eating enough were valued for different reasons, such as social status or personal freedom. Fashions also reflect these views of food and beliefs about body size.

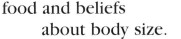

This woman wears a bathing suit from the early 1900s. A woman's body naturally stores fat in certain places, giving her a curvy figure.

For apples and pears
Bodyshape and size is determined by many factors, such as genetics, or the characteristics we inherit from our parents, and our sex. Women are often described as "pear-shaped", meaning that they store fat on their hips, and men are said to be "apple-shaped" because they store fat around their waists. This is not always true, because each person's body is different.

For health and fitness
Today, doctors encourage a healthy lifestyle. This means exercising, taking care of our health, and eating a balanced diet with a variety of different types of food. Vitamins and minerals are very important. It is possible to get all the nutrients we need from fresh foods but many people take vitamins because they do not eat a balanced diet. It is better to eat well than to rely on vitamins in a bottle.

As a sign of equality
In the 1920's many women had boyish figures. During World War I, men were off fighting the war and women did more of the physical work at home. This made their bodies stronger. Food was also scarce and as a result, people were less fat. After the war, many women wanted to keep this boyish look because they wanted the freedom, rights, and respect that men enjoyed.

The woman wears fashionable clothing of the 1920's. She has a short, boyish haircut and a slim figure. Her clothes do not emphasize her feminine figure as clothes had done in the past.

Is a business

The fashion for certain body shapes is strongly effected by the fashion in clothes. Certain clothes look better on a fuller figure, while others suit a thin figure. Popular fashion magazines encourage readers to diet to fit their bodies into the latest styles. Diets go in and out of fashion and large amounts of money are made by telling people what kind of body they should have.

As social status

In some cultures and at different times in history, being fat was very desirable. A fat body was proof that a person had money and high social standing. Wealthy people were fat because they could afford to eat a lot of food and did not have to do physically demanding work.

Rubens was an artist who was famous for his beautiful paintings of curvy women.

Suits a job

Many people do jobs or have hobbies, such as sports that require them to be physically fit. It is also common in the modern world for people to work in offices, sitting down all day and doing little exercise. These different activities demand different diets. Ideally, the food we eat should suit our lifestyle so that we have plenty of energy to perform tasks.

Many people in developed countries like to spend some of their free time playing computer games. This can be good fun, but if we spend too much time sitting still, we don't get enough physical exercise and risk damaging our health.

Pressures

At different times in history, both men and women have felt that they should control what they ate to conform to fashionable body shapes. In modern western society, this means trying to stay slim, and "watching your weight" has become a common phrase. People come in all shapes and sizes, and weight is affected by many factors, including ill-health, genetics, and exercise.

Today, people often weigh themselves on a bathroom scale.

As a moral choice

The diet a person eats can sometimes be based upon religious or moral beliefs. People choose not to eat certain things because it is a part of their religion, such as the **Kosher** laws followed by many Jewish people. Sometimes, a person chooses not to eat certain foods because of their own moral beliefs. **Vegetarians** do not eat meat. They believe it is wrong to eat animals.

This Jain priest, is a vegetarian. He follows his beliefs so carefully that he wears a mask so that he does not inhale a fly by mistake.

Can be red hot

Some vegetables and spices, such as chili peppers (right), contain natural substances that make your mouth feel very hot when you eat them. Dried or fresh chili peppers are widely used in many countries, including India and Mexico, where they originated. It is easy to become addicted to hot foods, because they make our brains release chemicals that make us feel good. Hot foods are also useful. They make our noses run and, when we have a cold, this makes it easier to breathe. Ointment made with chili peppers is also used to ease stiff or sore muscles and joints.

Come from olive oil

Olive oil is made from the crushed, or "pressed" fruit of the olive tree. There are many different varieties, all with their own color and taste. Some oils are light and pale yellow; others are thick, strong-tasting, and deep green. All contain a type of fat that is very good for our health. Olive oil has been a part of Mediterranean and Middle Eastern diets for thousands of years. The best quality olive oil is taken from the first pressing of olives, without any added chemicals or heat. It is known as "extra-virgin" oil.

Color and flavor

The appearance and color of food is very important. Food that looks good tastes better than food that does not. Color is very important in making food look good. Red and yellow naturally attract the eye, but most people are horrified by the thought of eating blue food. The flavor, and smell, of food is just as important as its appearance. Over the centuries, cooks have experimented with a vast range of fruit, vegetables, herbs, and spices, to learn how to add delicious new tastes to food. Today, the ease of international travel has meant that many people now eat food that was once considered unusual or exotic.

Olive oil is spoiled by bright sunlight. Traditionally, it was stored in straw-covered flasks like this one.

From vegetables

This group of colorful vegetables looks good enough to eat! Vegetables are the leaves, stalks, bulbs, roots, and tubers of many different plants. The only thing they have in common is that they look attractive, taste delicious, and are full of minerals, vitamins, and fiber. All are good for our health. Vegetables are eaten in a wide variety of dishes. Most can be served cooked or uncooked, but some, like potatoes, should not be eaten raw.

Given by garlic

For a small bulb, garlic has a very powerful flavor and an even stronger smell! Garlic's use dates back to ancient Egypt. Today, it is traditionally linked to food from the Mediterranean region. Many people believe that garlic is good for the heart. Used raw, it is also a powerful **antiseptic** that can help fight viruses. Popular belief claims it also keeps mosquitoes, away.

From fruit

Fruits are very important for many reasons. They contain seeds that produce new plants. For thousands of years, fruits have been gathered and eaten because of their sweet taste. As well as tasting good, many fruits are also beautiful to look at. Their sun-ripened skins glow golden, pink, orange, red, and yellow, as in this still life painting (left) of apples and oranges.

Herbs and spices

Many of the foods we cook and eat are given color and flavor by herbs and spices. Herbs are the fresh or dried leaves of growing plants. Spices are the dried roots, bark, and seeds of plants. Herbs and spices usually come from different plants, although a few plants, such as cilantro, or coriander, provide both leaves and seeds. Herbs are delicately flavored, while spices are stronger and more **pungent**. For many centuries, the spice trade was one of the most important forms of international **commerce**. Spices from India and Southeast Asia were carried great distances to market.

Using parsley...

Parsley is one of the most popular herbs in European cooking. It has a beautiful bright green color and a delicate taste. It is often added, raw and finely chopped, as a garnish, or decoration, to a dish that is ready to serve. As well as looking attractive, parsley is also nutritious as it is packed with iron and vitamins.

Bay leaves...

Bay leaves are the glossy leaves of a small evergreen tree. Bay trees are often grown in pairs, in formal courtyard gardens, or on either side of a front door. Their leaves have a mysterious, slightly musky, smell that is used to add depth and richness to casseroles and stews. In ancient Roman times, crowns made of bay leaves were given to famous poets, as a mark of honor and respect.

fennel seeds

rosemary

basil

stone mortar and pestle

anise

cilantro/coriander

cumin

Seeds of fennel, anise and cumin are commonly used in Indian foods. Before cooking, they are crushed using a pestle and mortar, gently fried in oil to release their flavor, then added to curry. In Europe, rosemary is traditionally cooked with roast pork. Basil is a favorite ingredient in Italian pasta dishes. Cilantro, or coriander is cooked with fish, garlic and lemon grass in Thai food.

...And thyme

Thyme is a low-growing, bushy plant with pink flowers. It grows wild on mountainsides throughout Europe. The strongest tasting varieties come from countries where there is hot summer sun. Thyme is used to flavor roast meats, and is added to soups and stews.

Unmistakable onions

Prized for their unmistakable, strong flavor, onions are a favorite ingredient in many national **cuisines**. They originated in central Asia, and are now grown in many places in the world. Onions have been cultivated for thousands of years. Today, there are many different types, with different skin colors, strengths, and flavor. Onions are a swollen bulb that sits on the surface of the ground, and sends down roots into the earth.

This Chinese pottery tea set (below) was made in the 19th century.

From China

Tea is an evergreen shrub, with small, glossy, dark-green leaves. It likes a mild, damp climate, and grows well at high altitudes. The best teas grow only in areas where there is an ideal combination of rich soil, shelter, and sunlight. There are tea plantations throughout the south of China. The crop is harvested (below) in March or April.

The delicate leaves from the tip of each shoot are picked by hand during the tea harvest in China.

Stimulating drinks

People often describe tea as "the cup that cheers." For thousands of years, drinks made from plants mixed with hot water have provided warmth and comfort. They have become the center of many social rituals, from coffee breaks to religious tea ceremonies. Special jugs and cups have been made to hold them. People drink coffee and tea in many different ways. Unlike alcoholic beverages, such as wine or beer, most plant based drinks such as tea, coffee, and cocoa stimulate the senses without causing drunkeness. Some are even good for health. Chocolate drinks contain an important mineral called iron, which is needed to keep blood healthy. Some scientists suggest that drinking tea can protect against diseases.

As a status symbol

Tea became popular in Europe in the seventeenth century, especially in England, where it was drunk by people from all social classes and is still considered the national drink. In France, tea was never as popular, and was only drunk by people in high society.

This illustration shows a Japanese woman, dressed in traditional costume, taking part in a tea ceremony. For her guests, it is an honor to be invited.

This brass tea urn (left) and gong were made for a British family living and working in India around 1900.

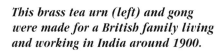

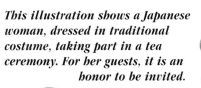

In tea rituals

The tea ceremony is one of the most important traditional rituals in Japan. It was first held by Buddhist monks between 1300 and 1500, and continues today. During the ceremony, the host or hostess serves tea to their guests with great delicacy, politeness, and precision. These actions are a symbol of the **Zen Buddhist** search for beauty, purity, and calm.

This painting (above) by American artist Mary Cassat (1844-1926) shows people drinking tea at home, using delicate cups and saucers.

For the Aztecs

The ancient peoples of North and Central America, the Maya and Aztecs, were the first to discover how to extract chocolate from cacao trees that grew in rainforests. They mixed cacao beans with water, honey and spices, to make a thick frothy drink. It was reserved for special occasions, for royalty, and for the gods. The word "chocolate" is based on the Aztec name for this drink.

This drawing from a Mixtec codex, or folding book, (above) shows chocolate being drunk at a royal wedding celebration, around the year 1100.

When coffee and cocoa were first introduced to Europe from the Middle East and North and Central America, they were rare and very valuable. Only rich families could afford them. They liked to serve these drinks in special containers, like this French 18th century silver and gold chocolate pot. It has a warmer at the bottom to keep the chocolate hot.

Fry and Sons was one of the first companies to sell chocolate commercially.

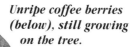

In America

Coca-Cola was first sold in the U.S. in the ninteenth century. Today, under the brand-name "Coke," it has become one of the world's most famous products. It is also one of the most advertised (above). Coca-Cola is a sweet, fizzy drink, made from a secret recipe. Originally, it contained an extract of coca leaves from the same plant that produces the drug cocaine.

From bean to chocolate bar

This early twentieth century advertisement shows cocoa powder pouring from a giant cacao pod, the seed of a tropical tree. Making cocoa powder is a complicated process. First, pods are split, and the beans inside are removed. They are then **fermented**, dried, roasted, shelled, and ground into powder. The powdered cocoa can be mixed with milk as a drink, or blended with cocoa-butter, the vegetable fat from cacao beans to make chocolate bars.

Unripe coffee berries (below), still growing on the tree.

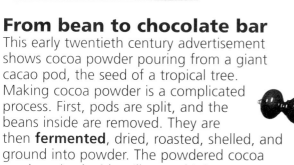

From bitter beans

Coffee is also made from the beans, or seeds of a tropical tree. Originally from east Africa, it grows in warm, hilly, frost-free countries all over the world. One of the largest producers is Brazil. Coffee berries are harvested, and left to rot so that the beans inside can be removed. The beans are dried, roasted, and ground for use. Instant coffee is made from fresh brewed coffee, with most of the water removed.

In cafe society

Coffee drinking first became popular in north Africa and the Middle East. It was unknown in Europe until around 1600. Soon after that, coffeehouses became fashionable places to meet and talk. Groups of scholars, **philosophers**, and politicians met to discuss the latest ideas and new books, and sometimes to sit in a quiet corner and compose new works. Today, coffee houses are still important meeting places for trendsetters. This woman (above) is drinking in a coffee house in Prague, Czech Republic.

Conserved

Animals and plants that live in the desert have evolved ways of saving and storing water for emergency use. Camels (left) store up to 24 gallons (90 liters) of water in the large fatty hump on their backs. They can survive for six to eight days without drinking.

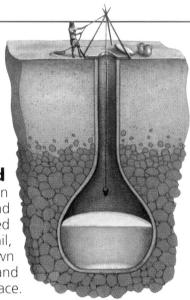

In ground

Where rocks and soils are suitable, rainwater often trickles through the surface layers of the Earth and collects deep underground. These buried lakes are called "aquifers." In many dry lands, where rains often fail, aquifers provide a vital water supply. People dig down deep to find underground water, like this well below, and use buckets or pumps to raise it to the surface.

Water

Our bodies are almost 80 percent water. Without water we would die, yet many people in rich countries waste water while gardening or doing household chores. In poor countries, water is even more of a problem. People in many parts of the world do not have clean, reliable water supplies. Diseases carried by water can kill. Many of these diseases such as **dysentery**, and **cholera**, can be controlled by simple sewage systems, public education, and clean water wells.

The ancient Romans constructed aqueducts, or raised channels, to carry rainfall from rivers to cities and towns. Many aqueducts were so well made that they have survived for almost 2000 years.

Carried for miles

In many parts of Africa, Asia, and South America, getting water from rivers or wells is a tiring, time consuming task. Millions of women, like these (right) in Mozambique, have to walk miles each day to get water. They carry heavy buckets of water on their heads and their babies in their arms.

For healthy bodies

Humans can survive without food for several weeks, but will die if they go without water for more than two or three days. Water helps all the organs of the body work better. Many doctors say that people should drink about eight glasses of water every day, and more if we are doing exercise like this cyclist (left).

To purify the soul

Water is often used in religious ceremonies, as a sign of purity and holiness. It washes away past **sins** and troubles. Followers of the Hindu faith in India honor the waters of the Ganges River as a symbol of divine life. They bathe in it, and when they die, are **cremated** beside its banks.

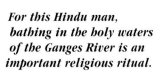

For this Hindu man, bathing in the holy waters of the Ganges River is an important religious ritual.

...And firewater

Strong alcoholic drinks are sometimes called "firewater". Unlike pure, fresh water, they have a harmful affect on the body. Doctors think that a small amount of alcohol may protect against heart disease, but they also say too much alcohol is very bad for health. Alcohol slows down the brain, strains the heart, and numbs the senses. It increases the risk of cancer, and can eventually cause liver failure and death.

In the past

Until the twentieth century, many water supplies in Europe were not safe to drink. There were some alternatives, such as whey or buttermilk, the liquids left behind after milk was made into cheese or butter, but often people drank alcohol, even for breakfast! The beer and wine they drank was not as strong as they are today. They were safer than water because the brewing process, and the alcohol, killed germs.

Modern wine making is a highly skilled process. Many thousands of different kinds are produced.

Distilled illegally

From 1919-1933, the production and sale of alcohol was banned in the U.S. Those years became known as "Prohibition." Many Americans refused to accept the ban and made alcohol illegally or visited bars, called "speakeasies" where illegal drinks were sold. Around 1930, two police officers (left) were photographed beside this illegal still they had seized.

Turned into wine

For thousands of years, wine has been served at celebrations. Offering it, and sharing it, have been symbols of friendship, peace, and love. A well-known **Bible** story tells how Jesus performed a **miracle** to turn water into wine, when he was a guest at a wedding and the host's supplies ran out.

Found in the desert

This man (below) from the San people, who live in the Kalahari Desert in southern Africa, is sipping water trapped in a tree trunk through a hollow stem of grass. People who live in the desert are experts at finding water. They know where underground streams and rivers flow, and which plants store water in their roots or fruits.

Wine is made from crushed grapes and skins. Natural yeasts on the skins turn the sugar in the grape juice into alcohol. This wine maker (below) puts grapes into a wine press.

Brewed into beer

This party goer (above) is enjoying a mug of beer at the "Oktoberfest" beer festival in Munich, Germany. Beer is brewed from grain mixed with pure water. Sometimes, flavorings, such as hops or fruit, are added, then the mixture is left to ferment. Tiny plants called yeasts eat the carbohydrate in the grain, and give off alcohol and carbon dioxide gas. The resulting brew is strained or filtered, then bottled and stored.

These Aboriginal people in Australia (left), painted in the 18th century, are cooking and eating around a campfire.

Around the fire

People in some cultures still follow ancient traditions. They gather around a fire to eat, just as their ancestors did. Meeting for meals around a fire brings members of a group closer together. The fire also provides warmth and heat for cooking, and helps scare **predators** away. Many people, who normally cook on modern stoves, also enjoy campfire cooking at barbecues, or on camping vacations.

Standing up

In the past, many people ate one or two main meals per day, seated at a table with their family or friends. Today, eating habits are changing. Many people prefer to eat several small snacks, at different times of the day or night. They munch these sitting at their desks in offices, traveling in their cars, or standing up in cafes or roadside food stands.

Ways people eat

There are many ways of preparing, serving, and eating food. These ways depend on culture, religion, history, and the availability of food. For example, many Muslims follow the example of the Prophet Muhammad. He, like most other Middle Eastern people living over 1,000 years ago, ate using the fingers of his right hand. Technology has also had an impact on the ways people eat. For thousands of years, people ate with their hands until cheap metal knives, forks, and spoons were produced just a few hundred years ago. Meals, and the number of people eating together at meals, varies throughout the world according to local customs.

Customers wait to buy food from this snack stand (above) in New York. Many busy people in the city eat on the move, rather than sitting at a table.

Lying down

At feasts on special occasions, the ancient Greeks and Romans ate lying down. They reclined on their left side on couches, leaving their right hand free to eat with. Three diners usually shared each couch. Roman men and women ate together, but Greek feasts were for men only, although male diners were often entertained by women singers and dancers.

This illustration shows Muslim men saying prayers of thanks before the beginning of a feast. In some Muslim countries, men and women do not eat together. Men are served separately.

This picnic basket (right) was made in Europe in the late nineteenth century. It contains everything necessary to carry and serve an elegant meal for two, including fine china and silver-plated cutlery.

On the floor

Seating arrangements for serving and enjoying food vary around the world. In many parts of Asia and Africa, meals are eaten sitting on rugs or cushions on the floor. In Europe and North America, most people prefer their food to be served at a table, and to eat while sitting on a chair.

Outside

Working people have always eaten their meals outdoors, in fields or vineyards, or on building sites. Picnics, meals eaten outside for fun, are also popular among people who have the time and money to spare for leisure. They pack up food that is easy to eat, and carry it to a scenic area. Favorite picnic sites include shady woods, grassy fields, or by a river, lake, or ocean.

In Japan, serving food can be a work of art. This plate (right) of sushi, seaweed wraps of rice and raw fish, looks almost too beautiful to eat.

Chopsticks

In many parts of East Asia, such as China, and Japan, people eat their food with chopsticks. Chopsticks are two long, slim pieces of bamboo, wood, or metal, that gently taper towards one end. They were invented thousands of years ago. Diners hold both chopsticks in one hand, and use the tips to carefully pick up bits of food. It is poor manners to wave your chopsticks around, or to point them at anyone.

This painting (left) by British artist William Hunt, is called "Christmas Pie." It shows a cheerful boy about to eat a huge pie, with his knife and fork at the ready.

With their hands

In many parts of the world, people do not use knives, forks, or spoons, or eat off plates made of pottery, wood, or metal. Instead, it is traditional to eat using the fingers, and serve food on "plates" made of large, shiny leaves, such as the leaves from banana trees. Almost always, food is eaten using the right hand only. The left hand, traditionally used for washing, is considered unclean.

Using a knife and fork

Sharp metal knives have for thousands of years, been used for butchering meat and preparing food. Spoons have also been widely used since at least ancient Egyptian times. Forks are a much more recent invention. They were not used for eating meals at the table until the late Middle Ages, around the year 1400. In the past, tables were not set with cutlery as they are today. Instead, diners brought their own knife, fork, and spoon with them.

This woman (left) from India sits beside a dish of food which she has just cooked. She will eat, using the thumb and two forefingers of her right hand, which is a local custom.

Glossary

Alimentary canal: The digestive tract or system through which food passes and where digestion takes place. It extends from the mouth to the anus.

Altar: An elevated structure or place where religious ceremonies take place.

Anoint: To apply oil during a religious ceremony.

Antiseptic: Something capable of preventing infection from germs.

Bacteria: Tiny one-cell organisms. Some bacteria can cause infectious diseases.

Bible: The Christian holy book.

Breeds: Groups of plants or animals with common ancestors and characteristics.

Cells: The smallest living organism.

Chemicals: Artificial and natural substances that can help plants grow but are often harmful to the environment.

Cholera: A deadly infectious disease that can be spread through contaminated drinking water.

Christians: Someone who believes in Jesus Christ as the son of God and follows his teachings from the Bible.

Colonists: A group of people who settle in a distant land but remain closely associated with their parent country.

Commerce: The buying and selling of goods on a large scale.

Commodities: A product, resource, or article for trade or commerce.

Communist: Someone who believes in an economic system in which the country's resources are held in common by all the people and regulated by the government.

Convenience foods: Prepackaged food that can be prepared quickly and easily.

Cremate: To burn a corpse.

Crop rotation: The successive plantings of different plants on the same land to improve soil fertility and help control insects and diseases.

Crucified: Put to death on a cross.

Cuisine: Food, or a style of cooking.

Cultivated: Land prepared for growing and tending crops.

Deity: A god or goddess.

Delicacy: A pleasing or appealing food for refined tastes.

Developed: Advanced in ability or sophistication.

Developed countries: Countries with advanced industrial capabilities.

Digestive system: The alimentary canal. The system responsible for the ingestion, digestion, and absorption of food.

Domesticated: Trained or adapted to live around humans, or in the case of farm animals, be of use to humans.

Dysentery: A disease of the lower intestines usually caused by bacteria or parasites ingested in contaminated drinking water.

Eating disorders: Potentially life threatening conditions associated with food, such as anorexia, nervosa, or bulimia.

Exotic: From another part of the world. Foreign, unusual, or different.

Extinct: No longer existing or living.

Fermented: Food or drink that has undergone a change in composition from the introduction of yeasts, molds, or bacteria. Wine is made from fermented grapes whose sugar is converted by yeast.

Fertility: The ability to bear children, or the birthrate of a population. Also, the ability to produce things. When soil is fertile it is good to grow crops.

Fertilizers: Synthetic or natural materials, including manure, that are spread onto soil to help plants grow.

Genetically modified (organisms): Individual life forms with altered genetic makeup (DNA)

Individual: A single person, animal, or plant (one).

Kosher: Jewish dietary laws.

Lord: A man of high rank. Often someone who owns land that peasants farm.

Miracle: An event that cannot be explained by nature and is assumed to be an act of God.

Muslim: A follower of the religion of Islam and the teachings of the Prophet Mohammad.

Nobleman: A man of noble rank or class.

Nourishing: Providing with food necessary for life and growth.

Pagan: One who is not a Christian, Moslem, or Jew.

Pesticides: Chemicals used to kill pests, especially insects that harm crops.

Philosopher: A person who lives and thinks for the pursuit of knowledge and wisdom.

Pilgrims: English colonists who settled in New England in 1620 in order to follow their religion freely.

Predators: Animals that live by preying on other animals.

Preservatives: Something used to preserve food, especially a chemical added to prevent spoilage.

Priestesses: Women religious leaders who perform pagan rites.

Processions: A group of people, vehicles, or objects moving along in an orderly fashion.

Pungent: Strong, sharp taste or smell.

Roman: Something relating to the people or culture of Rome.

Saint: A holy person in some religions.

Saliva: The watery mixture of secretions from the mouth that lubricates chewed food and helps people to swallow.

Sins: Offenses or violations.

Spiritual beliefs: Beliefs of the soul, religion, faith, or god.

Staple: A basic dietary item like flour, rice, or corn.

Sustainable: The ability to maintain things over a long period of time.

Symbol: Something that represents something else by association. The flag is a symbol of a country.

Tanned: Processed leather from rawhides.

Third world: Countries that do not have enough money to develop resources, the economy, or even feed all of their citizens.

Torah: The Jewish holy book.

Utensils: Forks, knives, spoons, and other items used to cook or eat food.

Vegetarians: People who do not eat meat.

Zen Buddhists: A Chinese and Japanese school of Buddhism that says enlightenment can be attained through meditation and self contemplation rather than faith and devotion.

Index

Acknowledgments

The publishers would like to thank the following picture libraries and photographers for their kind permission to reproduce pictures:

t=top; tl=top left; tc=top center; tr=top right; c=center;

cl=center left; b=bottom; bl=bottom left; bc=bottom center; br=bottom right

Marco Lanza: p8tr, 8bl; p 9c, br; p 12cr; p 13tl; p 17tr, 17cl, 17br; p 18bl;
p 19tl, 19tr, 19br; p24cr; p 26tr; p 28; p 29cl, 29bl, 29br
Giuseppe Carfagna, Roma: p 11c
Scala Group, Florence: p 13br
Index / Barbieri: p 16cr
The Shakespeare Birthplace Trust: p 17tl
The Bridgeman Art Library / Overseas: p 17cr; p 30br; p 35bl
Panda Photo, Rome / R. Oggioni: p 19bl
Farabolafoto. p 18br ; p 21br
Marco Nardi / McRae Books: p 23br; p 25tr; p 34cr
Anne McRae / McRae Books: p 33tr